MUSK OX

Tom Jackson

Grolier
an imprint of
SCHOLASTIC
www.scholastic.com/librarypublishing

Published 2008 by Grolier
An imprint of Scholastic Library Publishing
Old Sherman Turnpike, Danbury,
Connecticut 06816

For The Brown Reference Group plc
Project Editor: Jolyon Goddard
Copy-editors: Lesley Ellis, Lisa Hughes,
    Wendy Horobin
Picture Researcher: Clare Newman
Designers: Jeni Child, Lynne Ross,
    Sarah Williams
Managing Editor: Bridget Giles

Volume ISBN-13: 978-0-7172-6259-5
Volume ISBN-10: 0-7172-6259-6

**Library of Congress
Cataloging-in-Publication Data**

Nature's children. Set 2.
    p. cm.
  Includes bibliographical references and
  index.
  ISBN-13: 978-0-7172-8081-0
  ISBN-10: 0-7172-8081-0
  1. Animals--Encyclopedias, Juvenile. I.
  Grolier (Firm)
  QL49.N383 2007
  590--dc22
                    2007026928

Printed and bound in China

PICTURE CREDITS

Front Cover: **NHPA**: Tom Kitchin and Vicki
Hurst.

Back Cover: **Alamy**: Steven J. Kaslowski;
FLPA: Michio Hoshino/Minden Pictures;
Still Pictures: Sailer/Schnizler.

Alamy: Steven J. Kazlowski 29, 30; **Corbis**:
Steve Kaufman 2–3, 37, Momatiuk-Eastcott
33, Kennn Ward 6, 34; **FLPA**: Michio
Hoshino/Minden Pictures 38, 42; **Nature
PL**: Nigel Bean 13, Niall Benvie 5, Vincent
Munier 41, Staffan Widstrand 4, 9; **NHPA**:
Kevin Schafer 22; **Photoibrary.com**:
Doug Londstrand 45; **Still Pictures**:
N. Benvie/Wildlife 17, Fred Bruemmer 18,
D. Harms/Wildlife 21, Steven J. Kazlowski 14,
Sailer/Schnizler 46, H. Schmidbauer 26–27,
C. Wermter 10.

Contents

FACT FILE: Musk Ox

Class	Mammals (Mammalia)
Order	Cloven-hoofed mammals (Artiodactyla)
Family	Antelope, cattle, sheep, and goats (Bovidae)
Genus	*Ovibos*
Species	Musk ox (*Ovibos moschatus*)
World distribution	Northern Canada, Alaska, and Greenland
Habitat	Arctic and tundra near glaciers
Distinctive physical characteristics	Musk oxen are completely covered in long, dark hairs; hairs on back are slightly lighter; the lower legs are also pale, making the animal look like it is wearing stockings
Habits	Live in large herds; feed during the day
Diet	Grass, shrubs, and weeds

Introduction

Winters in the Arctic region are fierce. It snows nearly all the time. An icy wind almost always blows, making it feel even colder than it already is. It's also very dark. The Sun comes up for only a few hours a day during the winter months.

Most animals prefer to spend winter away from the harsh Arctic weather, **migrating** south to warmer regions. However, a few stay in the Arctic all year round. The largest land animal to do that is the musk ox. Its thick coat keeps the animal warm and dry even in the coldest, bleakest winter weather.

A male musk ox has very thick, shaggy fur and large, curved horns.

5

Like goats, musk oxen are sure-footed in steep, rocky areas.

Giant Goats

It would be logical to think that a musk ox is a type of ox, bison, or another relative of cattle. After all, it has the word "ox" in its name. A musk ox looks a lot like these animals and is about the same size. Although musk oxen belong to the same family—the Bovidae family—as cattle, bison, and buffaloes, they are more closely related to goats.

Musk oxen, goats, and cattle are hoofed animals. They have a similar body shape and many of the same habits. For example, they have **horns** and they all chew the **cud**. That is, they chew all their food twice by bringing up mushy food, called cud, from their stomach. The cud is ground by the teeth for a second time before being swallowed again.

However, **biologists** know that musk oxen, though similar to cattle, are really more like giant goats. Musk oxen are extremely large. They have a short tail like a goat's and they are sure-footed climbers, too.

7

What's that Smell?

We now know that the "ox" part of a musk ox's name is misleading, but what about the word "musk"? Animals with "musk" in their name are usually a bit smelly. Musk deer and muskrats are known for producing a smelly liquid—and male musk oxen do the same thing. They produce a musky odor once a year when they are ready to **mate**. The smell is carried by the wind. When the scent reaches female musk oxen, they know the males are ready to mate.

Inuits—native people who live in the Arctic—have another name for musk oxen. *Omingmak* means "the bearded one." Looking at a musk ox's hairy face, it's not hard to see why Inuits call it that!

The male musk ox has an enormous hairy face.

A herd of musk oxen grazes on snow-covered plants on the frozen tundra.

In the Far North

The Arctic is not all dry land. In fact, most of it is made up of the Arctic Ocean. In winter the ocean is frozen solid. In summer there is still a lot of ice left—though some of it has melted. Musk oxen always live on land, on the islands and coastal areas of the Arctic Ocean. This land is called **tundra**. This flat, treeless land is always frozen beneath the surface. Few plants grow there because it is so cold all year round.

Musk oxen once lived on tundra all around the world, from Canada and Alaska, to Russia and Scandinavia. However, in the 19th century, people hunted musk oxen for their meat and fur. They killed so many that musk oxen were completely wiped out in most places. The wild musk oxen that survived now live only in Canada and Greenland. Some herds of musk oxen have been taken to Alaska, Iceland, and Russia in an effort to reintroduce them to these regions. So, they may soon roam free there, too.

Mighty Monster

Looking at a herd of musk oxen standing on the treeless tundra, you might think they are enormous animals. Without something to compare them to, such as a bush or tree, it is difficult to tell just how big they are.

Male musk oxen, or **bulls**, are slightly larger than the females, or **cows**. The tallest point on a musk ox is not its head, but the muscular hump on its shoulders. The shoulders of a large bull are around 5 feet (1.5 m) tall. That is about as high as a small car. Each bull weighs between 500 and 900 pounds (200–400 kg). The cows are generally slightly lighter.

Musk oxen have a large hump on their shoulders.

Musk oxen have a thick,
shaggy curtain of fur that
helps keep them warm.

Thick Fur

One of the reasons musk oxen look bigger and heavier than they really are is their thick, shaggy coat. The long hairs stick out from the animal's body, making it look much larger than it actually is. The coat is mostly dark, but there is a pale-yellow, saddle-shaped patch behind the shoulders on the back.

A musk ox needs its thick hair to keep warm. The long, shaggy hair also keeps biting flies and other insects away from a musk ox's skin. The hair that grows on the shoulders is curly, but most of the rest of the body is covered by long, straight hair. Some of the hairs growing from the top of the body are almost long enough to reach the ground. The long hairs form a shaggy curtain around the musk ox's body. This curtain is especially thick at the front of the body. On a windy day, the musk ox faces into the wind, so the thick chest hair presses into the body, helping keep out the cold.

Double Layer

Like many other mammals, the musk ox has a coat with two layers of hairs: an outer layer of long, thick **guard hairs** and an inner layer of **underfur**, or **fleece**.

The guard hairs are much thicker and longer than the underfur hairs. Their main purpose is to keep the rain and snow away from the fleece. The woolly fleece is made up of short, curly hairs that are packed closely together. Inuits call the fleece *qiviut* (KIV-EE-OOT). They use the musk ox's fleece to make clothes. Clothes made from musk-ox wool are about ten times more effective than sheep's wool for keeping the body warm.

Two layers of fur
keep this musk ox
warm and dry.

17

A musk ox keeps its ears close to the body to keep them warm.

18

Cold Feet

Most people find that their nose, ears, fingers, and toes get the coldest on a frosty winter's day. The blood vessels in these exposed parts of the body narrow to stop heat from escaping. With less oxygen-rich blood flowing through their vessels, these parts of the body can become damaged if exposed to the cold for too long.

Musk oxen feel the cold on their ears and tail, too. Like the rest of the body, the musk ox's ears are covered in a woolly fleece. The musk ox keeps its ears warm by pressing them flat against the body, out of the wind. It is often impossible to see the ears under the shaggy coat. Musk oxen have a short tail, so it can also be tucked snugly inside the fur. A musk ox's feet are kept warm by long, pale hairs that form two pairs of shaggy "socks" that cover the **hooves**.

Losing Their Hair

After a long, cold Arctic winter, a musk ox's fur coat becomes old and worn. When spring arrives, the coat begins to replace itself in a process called **molting**. The molt begins in April or May and takes several weeks to complete. In the middle of its molt, a musk ox does not look so good. Clumps of woolly underfur poke out from under the longer guard hairs, making it look very untidy. Eventually, the clumps of fur fall off. As the underfur falls out, it is replaced with new hairs. By July, the molt is complete. But what happens to the molted fur? The Arctic birds collect it to line their nests!

When it molts,
a musk ox looks
very untidy.

In summer,
a musk ox's fur
coat is too thick!

22

Heating Up

A musk ox's new fur coat is still very thick. It is perfect for winter, but the musk ox might find it a little too hot in late summer! Musk oxen molt only in spring and early summer. Their coat must be ready for fall, which arrives sharply in September. As a result, August is an uncomfortable month for musk oxen.

When you get hot, your body sweats to cool itself down. But musk oxen cannot sweat. They have only two sweat glands—one on each back foot—so sweating does not help much. To get comfortable in late summer, musk oxen climb to high spots to cool themselves in the breeze. That is not always easy to do because the tundra is a fairly flat area. The best thing a musk ox can do is to lie in some snow to cool down. That is if they can find any snow that hasn't melted yet! For most of August, the musk oxen have little choice but to "sweat it out."

Good Senses

Musk oxen are very good at sensing their
surroundings. Their wide nose stays wet.
A wet nose is more sensitive than a dry nose.
Musk oxen can smell one another as a result
of their musky smells. They can also smell
the odor of **predators**, such as wolves and
polar bears, from a long way off. Despite
their ears being covered by woolly fur, a
musk ox can hear well.

Musk oxen spend a lot of time in the dark.
During the daytime in winter, it is dark for weeks
on end in some parts of the Arctic. A musk ox's
eyes are extremely sensitive to light. That means
it can still see when there is little light. So musk
oxen can see well at night when the only light
comes from the Moon or stars.

Wanderers

Musk ox are wandering animals. They do not have a den in which they sleep at night. Nor do they defend a territory or have particular feeding areas. Instead, they feed wherever there is food and sleep wherever they find shelter.

In summer, musk oxen head for low-lying areas of ground. These places tend to have more fresh plants to eat because they are watered by the melting spring snow. In winter, the animals move to higher ground to find food. Highland areas tend to have more rocky ridges. The ridges sometimes shelter the ground and stop the grass from being covered by the snow. At the tops of hills, the wind also blows away some of the snow. In these areas, the musk oxen can often still reach the plants underneath.

Two musk oxen wander in the highlands in search of fresh plants.

Eating Their Greens

In summer, musk oxen eat whatever plants
they can find. The most common plants on the
tundra are small and fast-growing, such as grass
and herbs. Some of the herbs have unusual
names, such as bladder campion and fleabane.
Small plants find it easier to grow here. Since
they don't grow very high above the ground,
the plants are less affected by the cold wind
that blasts across the landscape. Looking around
the tundra you won't see many trees. They do
grow there, but very slowly. The most common
trees are willow, birch, and alder. However,
a tree that is one hundred years old is still only
3 feet (1 m) tall! Just the right height for a musk
ox to nibble its leaves.

A young musk ox chews on some willow twigs.

29

A musk ox calf looks for some tasty grass and leaves to eat.

Breaking the Ice

During winter, the tundra is covered in snow and ice. It forms a thick crust over most of the grass. Only a few patches of ground are kept clear of snow by the wind. Musk oxen use their wide front hooves to dig through the snow and expose the frozen grass underneath. But it's hard work to clear enough grass to eat. So musk oxen must rely on other food in winter. Taller plants, such as trees and bushes, stick out of the snow. The animals often gather to nibble on their leaves and twigs. Their favorite shrubs are bilberry, crowberry, and Labrador tea plants.

Sometimes in the depths of winter, the snow freezes in a thick sheet of ice, which makes it impossible to dig through with hooves. If a musk ox cannot find any bushes to eat, there is only one thing left to do: headbutt the ground! The mighty musk ox bangs its head against the ground to smash through the ice to reach the grass underneath.

Getting Horns

The horns of musk oxen are made from bone. The bone is covered with a thin layer of keratin. Keratin is the same material that makes up hair, hooves, and human fingernails. The horns start to grow soon after a musk ox is born. The horns are pale to begin with, but they turn darker with age. It takes around six years for the horns to reach their full size. By then, the pointed tips have been rubbed smooth, while the rest of the horn is still rough and ridged.

Both bull and cow musk oxen have horns, but a cow's horns are much smaller than a bull's horns. Cows also have a patch of fur between the horns on their forehead. Bulls have longer horns that meet and join together at the top of the head. The wide base of a bull's horns make a thick helmet of bone that protects the animal's head.

This musk ox bull has large horns that meet at the top of its head.

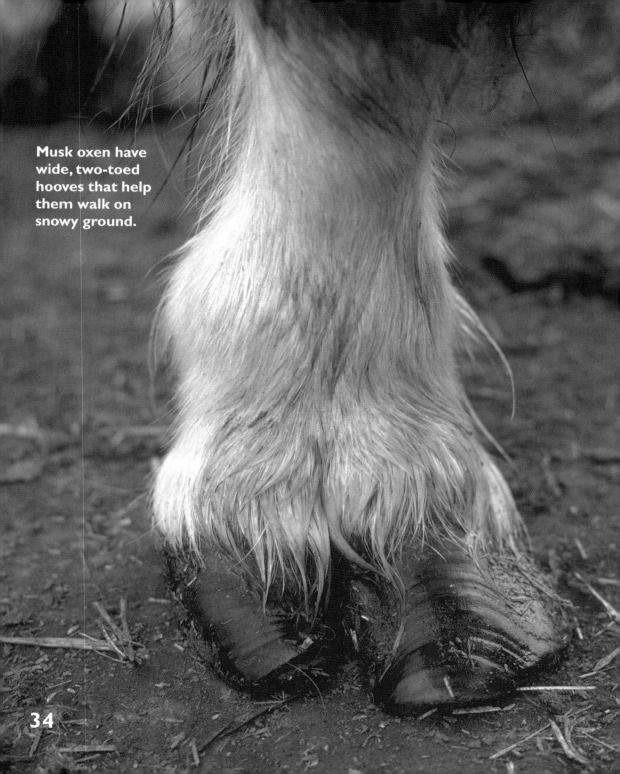

Musk oxen have wide, two-toed hooves that help them walk on snowy ground.

34

On the Hoof

Walking over frozen ground is not easy. The ice is slippery, and often the snow is very deep. Either way, it's hard to move without special boots. People use snowshoes for walking on deep snow or boots with spiky soles for gripping ice. But a musk ox does not need any of these things. Its hooves can handle slick ice and deep snow.

A musk ox's hooves are wide so they spread out the animal's weight, just like a snowshoe does. That stops the animal from sinking too far into the deep snow. Each hoof also has a sharp rim, which digs into the ice as the musk ox climbs icy slopes. The underside of the hoof is lined with rough pads, which help it grip slippery ground. In winter, the pads get some extra grip from small hairs that grow over them. These hairs also keep the musk ox's feet warmer while it stands on the cold ground for months on end.

Herd Instincts

You don't often see a musk ox on its own. They usually travel in groups, or herds. Some herds might have just three musk oxen. But most herds are larger and have around 15 members. Some herds may have 100 animals in them, but groups of this size are now rare.

The size of a musk ox herd varies. Musk oxen leave and rejoin the group throughout the year. The largest herds gather in winter, when several small groups come together. In summer, the winter herds break up as small groups set off in different directions to find food. The winter herds contain a mixture of bulls, cows, and their young. In summer, the small herds contain mainly cows and their **calves**, or young. The bulls wander between herds or live in small male-only groups.

A herd of musk oxen gathers on a beach in Alaska.

Musk ox bulls charge at predators to protect the cows and calves.

Circle the Wagons!

Most animals living on the tundra are small. They include birds, rabbits, foxes, and many types of insects. The musk ox is by far the largest beast to live on the tundra. It has very few enemies. Its main predators are wolves, which hunt in large packs. A pack of wolves will work together to kill even the largest musk ox. Grizzly bears and polar bears also attack musk oxen occasionally.

When an enemy appears, musk oxen defend themselves by forming a circle. The calves stand safely at the center. The adults stand facing outward, creating a ring of protective horns. Any attacker will have trouble getting through these defenses. But musk oxen do not wait for the predators to attack. The bulls take turns charging at the attacking animals. They try to trample the predators or stab them with their horns.

Freezing Fur

In the depths of winter, temperatures on the tundra can reach –77°F (–60°C). An icy wind whistles over the dark land, and even the furry musk oxen begin to feel cold. The herd keeps warm by forming a triangle. The larger bulls stand facing into the wind. They bunch together to form a wide line, making the base of the triangle. The bulls' hairy bodies form a barrier against the wind. The cows and calves stand behind the line of bulls to keep warm, forming the remainder of the triangle.

Musk oxen have no choice but to put up with the extreme cold. After a snowstorm, their wet fur freezes, and icicles hang down from the longer hairs. As the musk oxen move around, these icicles jingle like bells.

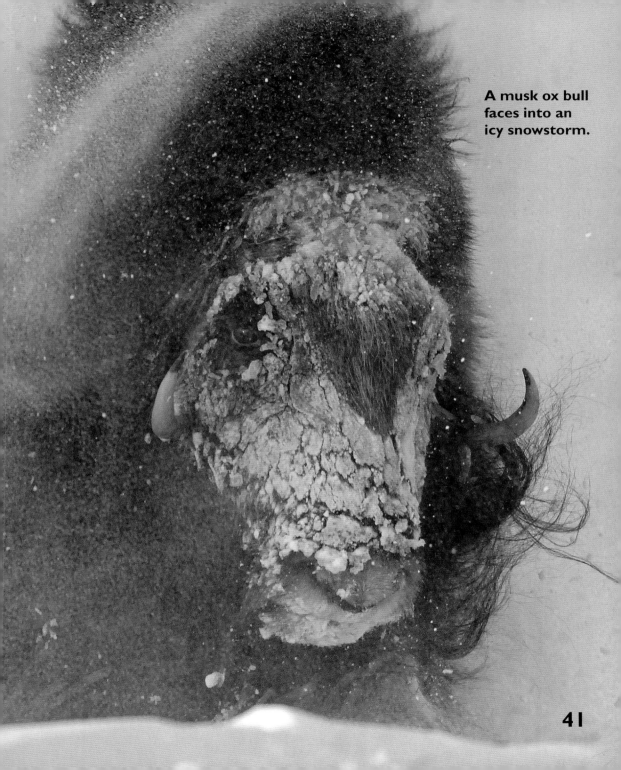

A musk ox bull faces into an icy snowstorm.

41

Two musk ox bulls fight for the right to mate with a cow.

Fighting for Mates

Musk oxen mate in early fall, just before the weather turns bad. The bulls show that they are ready to mate by giving off the musky smell that earns them their name. The odor comes from a liquid produced by a **gland** near a bull's eyes. The bull rubs the liquid onto its front legs.

Before a bull can mate with a cow, he must chase away any other males that have the same idea. The older bulls get to mate the most because they are much bigger and stronger than the younger bulls. If two bulls of around the same size both want the same mate, they must fight to see which one is the strongest. Musk oxen fight by charging toward each other and smashing their heads together. That makes a horrible cracking noise, but the musk oxen are not badly hurt. Their horns protect their head from damage. Eventually, one of the bulls gets too tired to continue charging and runs away. The other is the winner and mates with the female they were fighting over.

Spring Baby

Musk oxen cows are pregnant for about eight months—through most of the bitter fall and winter. When spring arrives on the tundra in late April, the cows are ready to give birth. There is still snow on the ground at this time of year. But the calves need enough time to grow big and strong before the next winter arrives. Therefore, that is the best time of year for the young to be born.

Most cows give birth to just one calf, although twins are also common. A newborn musk ox weighs around 20 pounds (9 kg). That is about three times as heavy as a newborn human baby. At birth, the calf is too weak to stand up. But after a few hours of drinking its mother's milk, the baby has enough energy to get to its feet for the very first time.

A musk ox cow stands guard over her tiny calf.

45

A musk ox calf drinks milk from its mother.

Mother and Baby

Musk oxen calves have shorter hair than the adults. They do not grow a long, shaggy coat until they are around two-and-a-half years old. Until then, the babies keep warm by snuggling up to their mother. The females keep their babies sheltered from the icy wind.

Musk oxen mothers have a calf once every two years. The females need that long to raise each of their calves. Although the babies grow fast, it takes a while before they are big enough to look after themselves.

The calf begins to eat grass at the age of one week. It will continue to **nurse** on milk for more than a year. After one year, the calf weighs nearly ten times its birth weight.

Game Playing

Children like playing games, and musk oxen calves are no exception. Their games are a good way to practice the skills they will need as adults. The calves play-fight by butting each other gently on the head. They learn to run by chasing one another around. They also practice defending themselves against predators by playing "king of the mountain." In this game, one calf stands on a mound, while the others take turns trying to take its place at the top.

Learning these skills will help the musk oxen survive for a long time. Most musk oxen live for around 20 years and have as many as ten calves.

Words to Know

Biologists   Scientists who study animals, plants, and other living things.

Bulls   Male musk oxen.

Calves   Young musk oxen.

Cows   Female musk oxen.

Cud   Swallowed food that is brought back into the mouth for chewing a second time.

Fleece   The woolly inner layer, or underfur, of a musk ox's coat.

Gland   A body part that releases a certain substance.

Hooves   Feet of musk oxen, sheep, deer, and many other animals. The hoof is a giant, thickened fingernail or claw.

Horns	Outgrowths of bone on the heads of musk oxen and many other hoofed animals.
Guard hairs	Long, coarse hairs that make up the outer layer of a musk ox's coat.
Mate	To come together to produce young.
Migrating	Traveling long distances in search of food, warmer weather, or a place to raise young.
Molting	Shedding fur and growing a new coat, usually at a change of season.
Nurse	To drink milk from a mother's body.
Predators	Animals that hunt other animals.
Tundra	Flat, frozen, treeless land in the far north.
Underfur	A thick layer of short hairs that covers the skin.

Find Out More

Books

Markle, S. *Musk Oxen.* Animal Prey. Minneapolis, Minnesota: Lerner Publishing, 2006.

Whitney, C. *Musk Ox, Bison, Sheep, and Goat.* Whitefish, Montana: Kessinger Publishers, 2005.

Web sites

Alaska Zoo
www.alaskazoo.org/willowcrest/muskoxhome.htm
Includes a special feature on the extinction story of Alaskan musk oxen.

Musk Ox: The Arctic — Wildlife, Land, People
www.saskschools.ca/~gregory/arctic/Amuskox.html
Find out about life in the Arctic regions of Canada.

Index